Gallery Books
Editor: Peter Fallon

THE FACE OF THE EARTH

Medbh McGuckian

THE FACE
OF THE
EARTH

Gallery Books

The Face of the Earth
is first published
simultaneously in paperback
and in a clothbound edition
on 7 November 2002.

The Gallery Press
Loughcrew
Oldcastle
County Meath
Ireland

ISBN 1 85235 319 8 (*paperback*)
1 85235 320 1 (*clothbound*)

A CIP catalogue record for this book
is available from the British Library.

The Gallery Press acknowledges the financial assistance
of An Chomhairle Ealaíon / The Arts Council, Ireland,
and the Arts Council of Northern Ireland.

Contents

*for Dr Dorothy Davis
and Dr Peter Curran*

Thou sendest forth thy spirit, they are created: and thou renewest the face of the earth.

Psalms 104.30

The Brood-bird

My encircler, I am placing a lock
upon my lips, though nine deaths
were in my unhemmed mouth
or thy mouth breast-white to my breast.

The tongue and knot and pulsing oil
of death without death goes round
in a thread, so I see neither the black
nor the white, tonight, in the upper chamber:

only the knee-woman, the world-woman,
the woman of songs.

The Face of the Earth

Now his private breath,
so easily pacified,
is in many ways an almost ideal
face, I have drowned in him
and his small elm coffin
of the English kind
keeps my vision in.

Our perfect and unmarked closeness
is a strangeness
that has made me sleepless
under a swarm of stars
turning the world into this world,
how it is what it is,
that it is what it is.

He was a bird which is not
in the habit
of sleeping on the sea —
not a sea-bird or river-bird —
a land-bird.
But no man killed by the sea
ever looked like that.

I caught myself reaching up
to his ear in whispers,
off the face of the earth,
in the field of the telescope:
I was afraid I could not
make a sound, that neither
of us was ever to hear
each other's natural voice.

I could not feel him,
and I did not know him
in his choice of that untempted
life, to bring his eyes nearer
to the mystery.

A deep ship moved
under his feet as she lay
cleared for sea, and slept,
her darkened sails
loaded with dew.

A flower showed
a little sail in the image
of the wind, dividing that moment
from the hour and the last flowers
we should see for the next
three months:

I am going to look
for land breezes
till the summer
when I should be whole again
to make his lungs consent
to draw air.

Mourning Engagement Ring

Airbrush out his cigarette
like an old black pot
put upside-down in a field —

he was barley,
the heaviest grain that grows,
a bead on the larger world
from my own intimate district,

a brother or a sister creature
of its ploughing edge.

How I have thrown a year away,
smiling a look at stars
in their dullest form,

and come back with nothing,
not even a birthname,
though I took his name strongly,

I over-rejoiced
in the achievement of that touch,
the toned senses of the controlled body.

It is a common word,
my very body,
my very mouth,

the same word for what is missing
or the small pieces of the field
which the plough has not touched.

I was so relieved to hear
those twelve strokes tightening
at pleasure,

the volume of conversation
in the restaurant,

I moved like string in a hem,
the stiff dark clay
prevailing in my hollows,

sown only on the chance
of rain with the dead that have become
the fallen, like stones set in wire:

a boy's anklet, pulverized,
his wooden bathing shoe, that runs along
the field lightly reploughed
and stirring.

The Worship of the Plough

Only old women like the colour
of deep water, when the body is thrown
into a running stream and becomes
the ghost of a childless person.

A coil of twigs brushing out
the sowing basket, like fluid opium
into a catch-basin, as soon as possible
before noon, before the rice flower forms,

drives the water full into
that absolutely level field,
a field left vacant in me,
well-white and smooth.

I go to the field by night,
to the place where the earth begins
to become moist, to a piece
of moist earth stamped and injured

by rain, like an animal black
on the shoulders. The helpless seed
is as much as can be carried
under the arm, the grain as much

as two hands can hold.
And if it is the bright half
of the month, time is a word
formed from action, measured

in Credos, or Pater Nosters,
an Ave Maria said aloud,
a Miserere. A plough is slightly
passed over the field, in a circle,

from corner to corner, and first light
waters the field's pulse
to its supposed extremities,
a hedge of brambles not fixed

in the ground. When the first
leaf shows, the overburnt blisters
give out little shoots which
weaken it a thread-breadth,

then a finger-breadth, till it is
two-thirds grown. In the marriage
of a grove to a well,
or a well to an image,

trees look their best,
half-wearing the produce
of one field less desired
if you weed your fields in me.

Ramoan Parish Bulletin

On the yachted sea
your boats burned so beautifully,
the last summer, as many of us then thought.

I unheard like a voice on wheels
your undersea eyes,
your snow, your snow,

the winter of endings
in your unprotected face.

The last time I sang to you
I said some words to the darkness
in a sabbath-dark bar
with the lights taken out,

using the earthquake
of my one and only body
to describe the earthquake
of my heart:

and I thought my huge
easy house was marked
by the ghost of my young father

striding on love's level
in this far, forgetful,
important place

outside that state of being
called his country,
my small bonebound island,
which world has gone forever.

There were trees being trees
outside, watching 'the herons
walk like woman poets',

a rush of strange mouths
named after the river,

and the time approached unshareably
that was leaving him behind

between the time when he was nothing
and the time when he was everything.

Love-spot

The old name of the glen means deep grass
and, passing through well-defended ghost stations,
another near-island in the island-studded river land,
its traffic once so light, is losing its island charm.

It has always been held that there is a gentleness
belonging to the abrupt hill looking down on settled land
and the narrow arms of the lough, an outlier
far removed from towns of consequence.

Music was often heard from it, and untimely deaths
attributed to the kind of spume collected there
and held in the air corridors of its clouds.
Nine counties can be seen from its summit

where the graves of three Danish princesses form
a rushy depression. There is no way to free it
until a key is found in the lake on the top
which is seen only once in seven years.

Although the lake is a holy one
it is death-reddened, part sweet and part
salt. The way the stones lie on the hill
is a dry waterfall of upturned cars,

an underlip of bronze-coloured glass
watering one face of a garden. My pre-war heart
felt it a sort of duty to visit the hill
once a year, as a former torture-chamber

that the crown offered any bright-countenanced
adventurer for the yearly rent of one red rose.
Sprigs of heather were worn during the fertile
hours on the hill and then discarded like the spring.

The pressure of fingers placed a bracelet
of bilberries as the sweetest food, the first
to scent cold air with flowers, on Candlemas
and Lady Day, and the other feasts of Mary.

One side of it is decorated with ribbons
and pieces of cloth, and often it deliberately
opens its autumn shirt to show the love-spot
on its left breast, or its neck, or its hand,

at the base of its cheek, changing its entire
course of well-mannered speech. But more often
it keeps the spot covered by a helmet
or a cap, like tongs across a six-weeks cradle.

Wild, inhospitable, ex-hospital of a mountain,
neither you nor the staggering horse are mortal,
as with no more strength than the froth of the river,
you burn in two and begin to widen the grave.

Understudying Envy

Grim silver, faint gold sky,
squeezing the last drop out of the day,
like a gate hooked back among bushes
and straining hedges,
give me your blackness, it won't
be watched or noticed.

I would detain the gestures
of the child you must have grown from
this side of the millennium,
your face of a known soldier,
the line of your baronial jaw
to look at fresh

when the fair harmonies
of body and soul break
very suddenly, seeming to turn
right round inside their skin;
so in five minutes a million things
happen and fifty years go past

in a second-earthy thought
or a sonnet upside-down.
The one to fall next moment
walks with a taking swing
hourlessly alight
to the nearest ship, *Cecilia*,

which will drift us through
or anchor us,
though the curve of the only world
lay a comrade dark between us.

Sky Farmer

I saw your fetch in the body-glass
fresh and fresh of the evening,
your own four bones and every rib of your hair.

You are not expected, you are given over,
you fell out of your standing
over your shadow and all your care.

Into your swans and the raven's book,
our lark-heeled linnet and blackbird,
that was first in a wood and last in a bog,

past grace, November-fellow,
where the plough runs into a globe-corner
over the rise of your hip.

About a mountain man's call below,
you turn the bothered ear,
the ten commandments of your shut hand

underboard, frost-stem in the gap,
your own, own silvern back now
in the eye of the bridge, a halter of snow.

Field Character

Mothlike, he makes the swallow look slow,
separating his flight-feathers as fingers,
closing the trailing edge of his wings
between beats, and his lyre-shaped tail,
from his old, cupped nest of leaves
to his later chosen, true, domed nest of reeds.

Often he merges with bark of fallen log
and insect-haunted least willow,
the song from his ivory banded bill
and robust beak almost a howling,
colder than a blackbird's,
lazier than a song-thrush's.

An almost song, even lark-like,
non-penetrative,
but a unique tearing of his rusty
breast-crescent, by his muscular tongue,
as when, shivering in courtship,
his eye-wattle raises his neck-ring.

Temple-sleep

In the flame-like rhythm of the wallpaper
a patch of scarlet takes belated shape:
an indoor tide of colour, echoing emerald and lilac,
as if you had set an aquarium into a window
so the sun would allow you to film all winter.

However long and charitable a delay
in the natural fall of daylight, such an alert
balance of red in its violet contour,
situated at last in its own appropriate world,
holds as much light as ever and softens

the enchanted fastness with a sense of spring.
Though the wholeness of the body was precious
in itself, the colour washes away the next few years
to a round dance in the background,
with a skipping and repeated backward step.

The bent head spreads like the gallop of a horse,
the hanging arm sculpts birds like a wasp
whose wings have been powdered with gold.
The sliced facet of the eye pulses gently,
its thin habit awaiting transformation.

It is when we are not trying to summon them
that we meet with perfect shadows among the wounded
dead, who return favours, by the luminous tracing
of their lowering feathers, the common radiance
and floral unfolding of anointed stones.

Reading the Earthquake

The sky was taken at a different moment.

Those rays that seemed to him to be
his new nature, his own sun-mind,
the rivulet of smooth silver
and the ridges of its body
that found itself a quarter of a mile
into the picture's understrength,

scarcely breathe with their one lung.

I found your last clear voice in him,
feeling you as a moving current
gentling his human essence,
the silked map of your eye
on the rose of his iris, looking at his hands.

I wrote letters by him to myself,
dividing you into ten equal segments,
from the top-viewed streets to the lurching houses.

The halo decorating his oval pupil
sponged away the numbness of your eyes:
you were the prevalence of white clouds
reaching him accurately and well,

the long, irregular, convulsive sound
in his sleep of the immediately following night,
and the wave of his poisoned life
lashing my horizon like a cast lance.

Making Your Own Eclipse

The word comes from a Greek word
for 'abandonment': we catch an untraceable
fire already kindled in another.

When night falls suddenly
for such a short period
in the clearest skies of the day

as a second darkening,
they could not have known
that what they were seeing was the Moon

acting as a screen.
For blue does not mean
its sensation in us, but the power

in it, the behaviour of the aligning
light in the pleasure-journey
of the obedient morning.

Across Ireland the blueness will drop
to temperatures of dusk,
a gentle east wind

will blow birds silent,
and stars along the Path
of Totality will decorate

the late forenoon.
Bleating flocks and fearful herds
will unexpectedly return to their stables

and patterns of light and dark
will tremble over the ground.
We will keep looking

at the fleecy space,
you curled up with your head
on my knee, saying, We

have been cheated, the twenty-
four seconds are passing and it
is much worse than we expected.

Then there will be the subtle
tension as the Moon begins
to creep into your face,

the cool band of air
in her shadow racing
about as close as it can,

to plunge into the gold spot
where the magnified Sun
will sail under the same perfect pearl.

Flowers will close their petals
while wildly thrashing magnetic fields
sprout from your surface,

so anyone standing near trees
will see thousands of suns
engulfing hundreds of worlds.

This will not happen again
until the year 2090,
but you must turn your gaze

as soon as the Moon starts to move
and stand with your back
to the black candle of the Sun

loosing flaming arrows,
like a plastic Christ that hovers
above a wishing well,

thinking, now it is over,
it was like recovery from a fever
which lasted about as long as is possible,

kneeling and raised as if washed
by the one planet where life is believed
to exist — hold your arms out towards it.

Viewing Neptune through a Glass Telescope

From my place on the coloured earth,
with my inner face of travel,
I could see nothing but the world as a whole,
our life of whirling steel

like a room composed in a quarrel
between covetousness and worship,
having an appetite for sounds
but no particular desires.

An aching fog walked through my flesh
from those homes created in space,
and the more streets I saw there
the less I had power to say.

What else could one do but walk
those same streets in their grip of summer,
succumbing to summer's little freshness
as tree- or sea-birds sing the hours?

Grey, white and lavender,
volcanic and feathery,
the layers of memory that surface
as one moves into tomorrow

so lately embodied,
whose meanings are not meant for us,
fed upon the water
that placard of light in the air.

Revival of Gathered Scents

Someone will tap a door
with just a single finger,
while beaks are still tucked under wings,

and the woman nestling
close to the blinds
has received a letter in the dark:

a knotted letter, snow-moistened,
the ink-seal on the outside frozen.
She tries to unfasten the rice-paste,

her sleep-swollen eyes aching
at the ink extremely dark
in some places, light in others.

The paper white as a flower
wraps up a single petal of mountain rose
whose dead white head remains

alone in the fields. It cannot
withstand the autumn's strength
with a cheap prayer,

expecting too many years.
The house is one where no one
cares about the gate,

and for a time the pond
stays as it was, the entire garden
is the same green colour,

and the two stars seem
closer than usual, fern on the tiles.
Now she has carefully scented a robe

of glossed silk, beaten and stretched,
with a pattern of decaying wood
and chrysanthemums faded in part

at the hems, yet she seems
perfectly clad, high-kneeling
to the God of Leaves

at the small half-shutters,
at the very edge of roofs;
because the tree, pear-skinned,

streaked with rain,
is divided into a thousand branches
full of curved promises

whose leaves do not change.
No next morning letter
attached to a spray of clover

with a long iris root enclosed,
clear-toned as the face a child
has drawn on a melon.

Glove-silver

When all Britain was dumb
with the chill of unbelief
there were tales told of him,
in his death-place, of the infant river,
by far-travelled and young rivers:
how the sparks of his father curved
into the west of the lake.

The peopled slope dreamed
of his woodedness, the slope
of the women saw slow-flowing
impressions of his body
on the low green shores.

Was he the corn, the storm-god,
the hill-god, the arch-druid,
the over-king, the seven times belovèd
buried standing upright in the hill
in his battle dress?

Or the agent of blight,
whose eyes were creels of turf,
the one blown into four quarters,
who would make one man
seem a hundred, from the one burned
fragment of bone missing from his heel
(small enough to be held on a finger)?

A figment conjured up from a place-
name, a word of unknown meaning,
a memory of paths,
it was his fatal light
and shape like a black sky
christened the townland.

It was his crossed spade
and shovel that opened the books
at church during the Mass hour,
and at the moment of Elevation
put beyond stonethrow the year's
growing between his adoring hands.

On the Feast Day of Mary the Fragrant,
Mary, the Long-living, the Three-breasted,
a day of commotion and ceremonial,
when they drown flowers below the surface
of uncanny water
and turn the chapel
mouth upwards for two harvests,
the sea's and the land's,

most Paris-like, my secret capital
becomes an upper-world husband
husked in the hand and kneaded
on a sheepskin, that day's milk
for the right arm of thirst

a bell of countlessness beside me,
and a child tossed on spears
by a clearer of forests
for early prize-lands,
whose heavy blood melts the snow
to a radius around him,
like a road made by demon-birds
and Angels of Pride.

Studies of Her Right Breast

Heavy breasts, they are the glistening
and densely set anima of the building,
startling you with their white flash
purer than the sky through white
rain-cloud. As a bird's head
is sometimes of one colour and its shoulders
another, they have a point of red
and a zone of white, a sunshine
whose light is white and its shadow scarlet.

Cloud throat, just where the petal
turns into light, clay that burns
or painted fresh air, sands of cloud
drifted under the breathing, they received
a deeper worship from the incense
of the sea, lake-sleep and ocean-work
shaping the clear-brown whisper of death
like an infinite thing in the soft
iridescence of their living tables of leafage.

Large stars, with distant effect on fields,
star after star whose many you belong to,
that nobody may ever miss seeing them.
Visible Paradise stung just enough
to eat it all up into my mind
touch by touch, a single clear touch,
a misplaced touch, whose finger is as fire
round the imaginary clock-face
of the eye-as-morning breast.

No decent calculable, consoled dying
in the angry pallor, all blinding-white,
of that strange, delicate and adamantine
colossal curve, its smooth surges,
and moonlike circumference all risen,

blanched and meagre, with the grazing
and resting in it of a coarse yellow
like sheaves of golden corn
fed with sun, the walls of sacred Death.

And oh, the world is keyless, both rose
and cankerworm, the one never separate
from the other, curdling wreaths yearning
for their bluest veins to kiss the gentle
processions to churchyards. We should
hold their foam-globes in divided drops
at our sword-points, pale, defiled
or furious rivers, ribbed with their Veronica
blue like fine-broken starlight.

And look to the snowy dome
of Our Lady of Salvation, of Safety,
moulding upon our imperfect lips
the low words of painted praying,
while others are blown away
further in flight, through the bottled
skies, wrecked and faded,
and wondering what the clouds
had been made so scarlet for.

The Fortified Song of Flowers

The eight-day clock moves on
not to be stopped, but our time too
is time — stained with culture,
we cover the winds with art.

The darkness is not purer,
opening its bomb-doors
to a carpet of night-offensive bombs
devouring the precious air

from the blast-proof windows.
The sudden linking of a number
of fires is golden-bedded
into the heat of a path

whose sun shall search the grave-hoard.
A bird will swathe its life-warm
head like a blade being bent
till point and hilt must meet.

Or else it is taught by the stars
to cry for the placeless dead,
to cry the name, to call
the buried by their song-cloud names,

though its cry always travels
against the stream, and few now
seem to be dying, branchless roads
blossoming draped by rainwalls.

Someone loves you with prayers
where a road is paved to church,
the flower of your oft-won mouth, hearing
your name inexplicably called out.

Navicella

A sunken street, air over ice —
how could the earth be jealous of the air?
Of movement and an open road?

Only your wings have survived,
a few dark openings,
your face in semi-shadow,

the pure gold or azure of the window
partially filled in
with dusted red ochre.

Flower between two abysses,
prisoner of your own image, or any wartime,
your head is somewhat difficult to read:

age-old, unconsummated
emblem of charity, only ever young,
which of these worlds is ours?

Your angels seem to listen
to what they are playing,
and can be readily imagined

passing in and out of doors.
There is a strong sense that the dark
doorway on the other side of the courtyard

truly leads into an interior.
Despite the number of words lavished
upon you, I would have to wear out

the word 'perhaps', because there is
no other way than studying
the wax and honey of your face

for hours while the sun progressed
from east to west, the blue straps
of your bible, your billowy mauve cloak,

the absence of punchwork in your halo,
your gestures set ominously to 'dead'.
Something else is always awakened

by the annulment of time
sweeping through the universe,
developing plans for travel,

his bewitching performance
making a Roman journey,
the harshness of his touch

stretching out his arm
in a powerful diagonal thrust,
by which he desanctified the world

in the snowfall of August 358.
A moment after being touched
by the golden spines of his crown,

all of these people were healed
by his shadow, that is no longer
a blue or golden void,

a rood screen, of eucharistic grapes,
but snowgrace,
healing with its shadow.

Image of Migratory Cranes

Thus they go past one another
in the adultery of the heart,
with the bravado of addressing light,
that chill on the unjust soul.

Falling somehow out of love
with the glorification of voluntary death,
one could talk about one's long walks,
seeing no harm, in the same breath.

Love songs are always a dreary flight,
which will not be love, the word
wearing thin and hymnic;
yet because I feel how much a word,

I often try to forget, Jean Paul,
the homily of your earlier self,
like gods that are really believed in,
your river-poems, driven out of the bud.

For eight important years,
years that will really count,
I will choose a new kind of agitation
that will not be one great grave,

but will not be unbeseeming
to the gothic study where you appear
sparingly, nowhere more, and never
thus, amongst everything used.

This Ember Week

It was my sunflower lifebelt,
the polished stone from the Bastille walls
I was rumoured to carry
next to my breast;

it was the number of years
I did not want to conceive
in my Carmelite bodice,
peony beads threaded
like a ring of seeds
on the white thread of my rosary.

A rock vibrates so slowly,
resonating with us at all speeds,
my turnover of bone
beaten for its ever-widening light,
flowed through to the point of breathlessness,
and would have lent patience
to the dead unsprayed in the wheatfield,
their primitive willow spines.

I buried my sins under an elder tree
to lose my burning perfume
beneath horses' swollen heels,
a bird-red wineglass at a time,
rubbing the closed eyelids
of my Christ-consciousness
with rosemary in wine.

The bitter receptors
on my mapped tongue
forgot the pagan name
of the wound-herb in the wound-drink
taken from camp to camp.

But one sinless flower,
a windmill-shaped grave plant
Shakespeare grew in his garden,
moon-unfolded,
lavender to crimson,
lavender to white, suffering
night adoration,

a state flower, or a flower
of closeness, that earned its common
name, following the path
of a leaf within an annual leaf,
the lip-herb lining your shoe.

Displaced to the Blue

Like a hall or garden planned or furnished
just to be passed through, I do not count
days when the moon's maximum and minimum
seem farther than my children from
their last birthday to their next:
the tenth of March is a down-turned room.

If an inch of time equals an inch of shadow,
and I think back, yes, through the slight
eccentricity of the moon's orbit, to the Sunday
we breakfasted on the North terrace —
was I pressing forward, did time open,
did it stretch from you to me as a roof across space?

What we called South then we should continue
to regard as the silent surface of water
were it not for the long days shortening,
and the day pattern shifting to night:
a twelve-hour day is innocuous, it merely
warms the leaf — but strong light,

knowing that 'this' is no longer 'this' or 'here',
casts leaf movement and stars on the ceiling.
And what could be more time-like,
after the coloration, the abscission,
of such a world-to-be-acted-upon,
than my one-way, accelerated, flowering response?

Sleeping with the Sea

Here light deflowered reflowers as the heroine,
as the heart no longer yours on your path.

Her hand of an extraordinary length
with blood in the underwood of every vein
papers your room in the broadest
of black and red stripes:

like a blind and exact hand
removed with grace from a clock
so the sensation of time, two drops,
is amplified into pages of stone
that disappear in the pure direction of number.

Almost hourly the extreme bud
of April's printing bows
to the current of the lowest form of life
in itself, then, warm as a soul,
develops in the world's dust
as though it were not there.

The murmur or crash of the waves, obscure
or decisive as the case may be,
are the only two words the stiff dreams
of the earth can remember;

the sea is made to repeat little phrases
such as 'the moon is pretty'
from all its wakeful windows.

August and the second half of the year
that has never lived either in me
or with me
re-opens eyes written

a distressing month ago,
to set out a child's clothes for a woman to wear —

for you, my superstition,
symbol of a movement more brotherly
than death,
who tarnish the flower,
whose clothes would fall to pieces if you moved.

Something Called Sleep

Sleep pours from a jug held at a height
in the angle of a hand, as the moon inhales
the world into which the present will soon fall.

Darkness takes the colour of colours back
from a much-shaded house to dawn's
great nakedness, breathing only once a minute.

Through the gossamer walls of a fourteen-year-old,
the long afternoons burn like a verandah
running along two sides with no interiors.

A month of mountains honeycombs the broken
spell of her breast, a week of windows lets them
more into her secret than they want to be.

I tap the table-mats sharply on edge,
a lady painted full length with the eyelashes,
her instrument, the last important flower of the year.

High Altitude Lavender

When snow fell for six hours
in an unforeseen direction,
the winter of fruit skins
recovered the footlight glow
of the sun as solid silver.

A gothic bouquet
of bronze-coloured roses,
standing up in military elegance
shackled to a trance,
flexed gleaming silken arches.

A stem of body-bound
orchids on a breathless postcard
changed their florid despair
to a midnight-blue glance,
and accepted to speak about next year.

A sheaf of country dahlias
in a communal ward
turned their humbled palms out
with morbid homage to embrace
the rustle of live wings.

I kept colliding with the absence
of my own heavy family,
fiery as this year's grapes
that the dew considered heartless,
as though they had grown deafer;

and addressed a conversation
to no one among us,
to the gardens framed by your windows,
that can imitate the shape of flowers
with their mere mouth and their empty fingers.

Melisma

His right hand cupped behind his ear
as he sits crouched, fingering a piece
of wood, is white as Circe's palace.
The film passes him by at a distance
like a mourner hiding from the end
of the light, as if its framework
wished to take prisoner the time
that had flowed freely, earlier on.

The piece is full of sunset, with traces
of the very oldest things, speechlessly nature,
in a three-quarters darkened hall.
Then, with an interplay of diamonds,
the moon soothingly makes its entrance
and, self-contained as the entry of March,
it moves forward inexorably
without looking vertical or back.

A breathless breath amidst events,
image of something without images,
it goes to such heavenly lengths
in its unprecedented transparency
that a path leads up from the core
of his nature, even in this field scene,
or we just follow where his voice goes,
listening on crutches that are shy of sounds.

He offers the gold in his throat
for sale in the market place —
the inhuman beauty of his voice,
its musty inwardness like a clarinet
passage, as though its overleaf of music,
his for the asking, needed consoling,
or we could be comforted by open
sound which has not been imprisoned.

At every moment we have the togetherness
of a congregation, feeding on our belief
in sound itself, be it absent or damaged sound,
that is still brazen with his hired song.
When the temperature falls so dramatically
all older music seems an ocean
of subcutaneous and iridescent sounds,
keeping us chained to the city of his —

merest presence . . .
which was the last thing the story wanted.

The Change Worshipper

We came to anchor beyond memory,
standing on gradual reddish tiles
flaming back at a low red sun:
if this were indeed a room,
if the universe is paved with it,
all over into gold, the light-sprinkled
hall folded the sky up like a scroll.

Even the window-blind was not
a simple muslin blind, but a painted
fabric-roof that permitted twilight
with a design of castles, and gateways,
and groves of trees and several peasants
taking a winter-bright walk
though the sun furnished the day.

To see his home put before me
was to hold a lighted match
inside my hand, a spray of red
berries in an opal pin in my coat.
My dusk was noonday and the day
without evening, for he was all
daylight and his own repose.

To find him truly at his leisure
within his today, his governing lifetime,
was some living-apart-together
like the boom of a warmed Atlantic
at the very tip of the Bosphorus.
My earth-imbalanced voice
posted a sentry before my lips

that snapped it like a spell
after he had found it,
a world to stretch the remotest

fibres of his senses in,
that could grow without changing,
its virtues wandering alone,
but extending their arms forever.

It was not to get the heavens
into his head I put my question
to the earth, that has at its heart
a collision. He no longer lays
his ear to the weapon of my lips
(and he cannot lay his ear to my heart),
but with the lips of the spirit, sparkling, he drinks.

House with Its Own Island

It is now running into more than a week
of shine without heat, of something said to me
somewhere in a branch-cluttered side street.
My sleeping was only so-so, and I didn't know
where my feelings were, to hurt the rock-part
of them, the most deceptive curve
of my sickness with sickness
so true to its winter self.

For many days I wasted daylight
wishing for an extra moon, and trying
to get used to it enough to use
and keep it, almost wastefully alone,
in the spending day, in the doubtful
chair, in the furrows of prayer
that were blowing up my minutes
like voluptuous-to-be
disappeared-into lips.

My friend of a year, it was the worst year
I have spent on earth, not having realized
you were on earth, noticing eyefully
the unconsidered land and the shooting-up root
happening to me in March. You lay in
with your whole body like an archer,
not in water either, but closing out the houseful,
the carpets, hangings, porringers and dishes,
all the number of my pewter platters.

Flame propping up my underflesh
and weary weathers anchored one end
of the bridge like a pair of thoughts
unsettling a book, some story
of something done with it:

you could protect the hours you liked best
seasoning the summer-deserted road,
living too high for me to have heaven
over with, reproving my wistfullest,
boat-worn, out-of-love return.

Thunder: Perfect Mind

My skin feasts as if fresh from childbirth
between clothing and prayer.
I am still thinking, I can withdraw
with a gentle drawing inward,
what a long way I have come
to meet him half-secretly
in his unfinished house.

It is no easy task
to turn on that shadow,
that ray of darkness with a whistle
so gentle, I say, 'Invite',
but I could say, 'Welcome',
resorting to touching
the objects he touches.

Where will the warmth come from in this,
if we are talking with nothing warmer
than the voice with the darkness
blown away?

He is intact, his house in order,
he gives it a light so far above
the never-goaded, cold part of his mind.

Valentine Not to be Opened

As into young sleeps old rain washes
with its lovely assault, trees in February
cry out with a kind of relaxing
for remembrance or prayer, inclining to the earth.

The art of spring is a bloodless affair,
always romantic to us, never to itself;
light burns so heavy it loses colour
but seems to want to be there,

to be coaxed out, like a mind within flesh
to flesh without mind. Our rye field
that was mortgaged (my kitchen
I think I called it) omits the season.

Even the farmhouse is without windows,
and no cloud nests in it. The cup from which
I drank is unnumbered bits
of a bigger story, smeared by my lips.

Let me arrange that pillow in your own words
you wrote with that spirit pen, to make
your exit easier, including the arms you held
above your head as you were breathing out,

or deep stroke the waist of your foot
with some almost contemporary touch,
incursion of the road into the field,
misenveloped wayfaring tree.

The Back Causeway

You lie near me, first ghost,
a third of a mile south,
a few rods to the south-east;
your soil is far from the best.

When I think I have met with you
I just count an autumn less.
I unbaptize myself your bad seed,
I rent my bed-life like a cow's grass.

It is my language against your superscription,
my stolen, silent sowing of poached
and smuggled 'All's wells', till the sun
enters Virgo, unannounced as your arms' farewell.

The Dance Garden

There is something moving on the window,
like a re-dedication that darkens all I have written:
there is someone shaking the wind flower
and the club moss like an arm outside the bedcovers,
a fever that strikes between seven
and eight in the evening, a midnight headache,
a twilight sensation of weight on alternate days.

Exhausted with your sleep-inducing voice,
I put on the saddest music I can find and cast about
for other voices easily refreshed
by sleep. Bubbles rise and diffuse
from my washday hands. Your flush
is dull to me, your yellow jasmine eyes not
a little injected, blind from the marking-nut.

I am struck by the horizontal line
dividing your lower eyelid in two. Can you see through?
It gives your autocratic face a fine
congested or besotted look, your wild indigo
lips are dusky all the time,
with small trickles of cold. Your scenery comes and goes;
outside you is the pure, undated space that you enclose.

There is no place for the half-real half-
language: your liveable field is the only open-eyed reality.
From moment to moment it changes, hops have
flavoured now its end stage condition; the image of antinomy,
yarrow, marsh tea, drosera or sundew,
the laborious dreams of thoroughwort, the more shadowed
    entry
of poison oak and monkshood release with their names
    what was empty.

Spoiled Muse

My love, my godlet, was unravelling the green
numerals in a red pagination. De-selfed,
he would send the most words possible, even
turning the page through ninety degrees,
trying to move more air so my warmth
would relieve his iced-over offscourings.

A sea-quake through a plain from which the sea had
withdrawn upwelled a thread of water
during the hours entangled in the clocks
to bewitch the brittle blue flower of flowers,
the flowers that live at these heights,
out of their rose-white angled houses.

Like eighteen-button evening gloves, they seemed
to open happily, though always asleep, and drawn
into themselves as a night-table, or carved
rifle-handle, or a widower's bedroom grate
outside on the grass, where their eyes ate
beauty, undoing the colour which is now light-brown.

The Water Guardian

Infields
under thatch.
A beck and call
visitation;

matter out of place,
an egg dancing
on a pure, plank floor:
cobweb courting the night.

Steward rather than owner
of the moor meadow
you have used for meadowing,
to break or stir the soil

so bared by burning,
would be to over-shoulder throw
the earth that has received
the great heat of his mouth.

Marble rats nibble
marble bills
in the timbered world
he framed like a disaster print:

a world of beds and tables,
within its girdle of common water.
A school of sorts, a kind
of preparation for the sea.

You sit in all your senses
like a thrown chair
as opposed to a joined oak,
turned on a lathe,

made of ash or elm
in a revolving frenzy,
triangular rather than foursquare,
open not closed.

Elizabethan or Bobbin chair,
thirteenth-century Byzantine,
neither smith-made nor mill-made,
between sun and sun,

even as the stork sleeps
with a stone in its claw:
where the sea arrests and beggars,
his remains, his standing remains.

A River Pebble

Though you had simply drawn
a thick line through the winter
and allowed the darkness to stand,

he was my ambition, my wildly
carved harp, he had kept
the brightness of violins out

by a chill of spirit
more than body.
His marvellously fashioned prayer

was a symphony growing
in his mind, a gigantic moving
garden of 'then' images

and wisps of melody
in the gentle paleness
of his throat tones.

A tunesmith opening
the velvety centre of the instrument
for the beautiful, skeletal '*E*'

blazed an entrance for the winds
veiled from afar, as prayers go,
in the heavens of Rome.

Christmas Eve Sky

On a day that cannot be anticipated,
half in the present and half in the past,
a rapid casting back of todays into yesterdays
is all that tells us we are seeing a path
through trees with a hill in the distance.

The sea, a strip of blue, aerated water,
receives its colour from the angles of two clouds
into its interior, as sanctuary and treasure trove,
all its feeling of open air, all equally lost,
like a star whose travels one wants to record.

My hand made a shining journey of its own
to its flowerlike, petalled head, too well kept,
whose resemblance is love, trued off with a knife,
its triple purity of fruit and glass already quite
radiant, rejoining the house that sparked it.

Soeur de Lait

Adorably cool, the buzzard
in a mint of light,
dropping out of sight
while still in this world.

I can testify that his voice
was steady, his hands
ringless and relaxed
beneath the linden-wood panel.

The zone of vegetation
was behind him, and all lesser
roads. They thronged,
burning perfume-papers,

just such a human compensation
for young, private perfumes,
so pitiful the carved frosting,
that were written in transparent Latin stars.

(*for Áine Louise, aged 8 months*)

Novena

The nightingale only sings for a few weeks
each spring, and in royal woods, unwithering,
not for provincials left in their provinces.

He would not call out his magicianhood
to our snowy orchard redolent of graves
or shrouded arrowy in the death-pangs
of the late roses;

his sheathed spirit would not break free
into its winged state on long light musky
evenings of common blue stained with fabled
raindrops to a spangled veil.

Mellow, distant, resigned, and mouthishly
fertile in unmeaning miracles, he uttered
black swanskin in the thin hours,
and tepid prayers embalmed by hope,
a bird-happy hope.

They were wonderful windows and stairs
of flamey air that spun me north again,
and held the oil-silk edge of my lips
to the fire as my life and in my life,

as a beginning of living, as a forever
and ever feeling.

But all sounds flinched together on horseback
when I sent my arm's warmth
into the red streaks of the stone
as a sort of dedication of the summer
or the distillation of two winters

following the softest conceivable
opening of his mitred mouth
like the short, slow flight of the kingfisher:

yet hearing the dead swell
of what he had actually poured forth,
his whole, stirred-up note, in that
torrent of letting-go.

Imagined Pastoral

A blue came to my mind,
as a certain blue enters your soul . . .
the result of remembered bouquets
long since dead;

those blue eyes, that mouth
shaped like a three:
the sky blonde, like honey,
turning blue with an infinite softness,

and this warm, black head,
its blunt and lucid black
against it — dark against
the steel-grey muslin background,

rose against blue. There was
the high light and the light
beneath it, a lightness which still
meets this need, a man caught

at the moment in which he gathers
his strength — you never doubt
that the tiny legs of a sparrow
can support its body —

a small blind arch in pale limestone,
its outer surface rusticated
by the interplay of air and wing,
only the most ephemeral movements,

those of water and air.
The horses gallop one by one
over him as in a dream . . .
the scrolls of his shoulders

are covered by the circle of his head —
the shoulder of the leg
on which he is mainly resting
is lower than the other.

His arms are like rolls of clay,
his extended upper arms keep
an olive-like fullness,
his forearms, like cords

for they can be twisted,
are tied in a knot, not loosely
interlaced: note how high upon his chest
they lie, those folded hands,

thumbs and fingers at the side,
lying there quietly like the hoop-handle
of a basket that has gradually
been lowered to a place of rest.

Cathedral body, cool but very bright,
white in this cooler shadow,
not broken as by a corner,
a pearly, opalescent colour all over,

with joints only large enough
to hold their bones. His foot
makes a line as sharp and straight
as a cut, though the foot, remember,

is a bridge, and those eyebrows
the wings of a butterfly preparing
for flight: the sort of music
written by the horse himself.

The Moon-spirit

If we were plants for half of our life
and animals for the other, she would be
two-thirds bird on her sleigh-bed,
naked with winter and cut to the bone.

She is wearing a dress of *lie-de-vin*,
the blackish red of claret dregs,
a necklace of wild mushrooms
and gazelle-droppings. Her sheets,

though woven from the flax
of her own farms, seem a chariot
made from the bones of the dead
held unperfected by the spell

of the earth. Gateway and vessel
of the sun, her silver-stemmed glance
over the moon-washed or the lamplit
wall is wide and magnificent,

as if the lighted dust of continents
to be, slowly decaying as the leaf
lengthens and air crumbles away.
She is surrounded by an English lawn

of old church land, a garden
without graves, its grass harvested
from beneath corpses. Her inflamed
mouth feigns breathlessness, counting

the months backwards on every hand,
and sounding them over, during the Advent
of this year swelling and sweetening
the undrunk glass of noble wine

she carries high in her womb
like my whole brother. A head sea
forsaking an old channel, her route
dark with the weight and sting of the water.

The Presence of Her Absence

When she squeezes tears softly
to manipulate the beyond,
I kiss at the unimproved road
and the spilt religion of her year-round
continuously dry iris-fold,
fluted along its whole length.

Its run-off moisture is a beautiful
weapon point at the window opening
of an old church, a wave pulse
in a lit-up, fishbone-lined tunnel
under a smooth sea, where fish
have designed their own eyes.

She repeats a word in an almost
touching way, and the words
that fly about the house all day
pull her backwards and forwards
in their daily pucker at the bird-
bone of her husk-confined ear.

As each page is read it is destroyed
forever, but I promise the next thing
soon, the pain-powder, the conscious
moon, the all-important lantern
with its overpowering warmth,
savage as her moment of waking:

a Sunday anyway, and the coming
and going part of the me
she is always with. Because we talk
nothing meaningful gets said,
except that something has to happen
which it never does

to the mound of clothing on the floor
of the room, the taken-for-granted
slimmest of gold bands.
I would give France an island
or two, this unique morning,
to be outside her sleep, not now.

Speranza

There is a war now to be fought
in her two-armed form: a cold
current only hours old
in her honeylike blood.

Spring reaches deep into her chest wall,
a deep, old, empty need
with no unspoken lines
and no words that are the wrong ones.

Lung pictures, white mould on leaves,
fractions of heart, the simpler bacteria
of meaning, slow her breath
to the tenderest of religions,

while a pale leafing voice,
burned clean, not yet awake from winter,
breathes her likely death into
my midnight-starved mouth.

Small View of Spire and River

The circle that her skirt, a brutal red
deliciously brushed, created barefoot
on the transdermal earth was my first glorified lips.

A host in white mourning which is said to have bled
was keyed into the solid and correctly treated
moon, as a field writing-desk is built into the top
of a gun-carriage, as a silver-bound pistol
is attached by a ribbon to a little stabbing bodice.

Her inward pulling was an ovary of fire
that sat on the skin of the unmoving world,
carving an embryo on the epistle side,
on the gospel side, to let the next spirit enter,
or let part of the spirit flee.

To protect her low heart from all this patching
and cobbling, she Irished me as the never-sick gods
visit us through illness, and braided this cord
like a felled tree into the mane
of my own child's first pony.

If daylight blessing the land deconsecrated
the gabled home of the sacrament sleeping seated,
or the intervening night only awkward angels
with terrestrial arms were singing
in a mosaic of muses, my soul covered her eyes,
my body paid the sounds she needs to make,
my father's ecstasy and clouds and the immediacy
of mountains in their vertical nativity
were the walls to my mother's ceiling.

The Gas Curtain

I am showing one of me to each eye
believing she is seeing all there is to see.

If her eyes are asked, they act
as if her body as a whole were moving
in some brilliant boat action
at the send of the sea.

I carry away her head and shoulders,
her existing eyes, yellowed but whole,
the crushed brick of her lipless mouth.

How curiously her body swings
to and fro, reduced to a mere
thread clothed with words.

A shadow often acts as the announcer,
and that small corruption in her
shadowed throat was an old promise

that time may be dropped
like a corner cut
out of the face she has lost.

Her bed half-opened and its clouds
exhausting anyone who walks there,
when her body closes does it close to all,
its curtain slanting boldly as you look?

The Journey Present

Half-light. They had lost half
their leaves. A shawl wound cripplingly
that she held together with her hand
willow-lined and snow-sealed her.

When the covers of her eye were lifted
from her heart so ground away with prayer,
like bitter flowers placed around wells,
a very light blue tear, so smooth

that it would slip unfelt into
her shoeless foot, thimbled her finger
and outsparkled the owner
of the prayer, a flower double,

or a flower thought black-staining
her sleeve, but coming to the brighter
street. Half-Buddha in her white
dress, black dress, she stretched down,

bent down like a beggar in her black
stoop, but never showed her fingers,
making all her movements a little late.
Her dance rained down on me,

her frozen dance of remembrance,
its silver dust into a deep shelf.
Words lightly spoken on the ends
of her lips in a blend of three lands

were weather sayings and the shapes
of sunsets on the shallow hills
that no wave formerly kissed asks.
The sound of the words was all I kept

of her, that bridge of nerves
between our voices, the boy name
and child name and clan name
that she dressed me in, the Traveller,

with the touch of a married woman.
What did it mean, the rough dried
yellow root cut of a loaf Mass
in an Irish mouth? A pit of old potatoes.

Then, to scent the cold air
with flowers, with that unearthly
fragrance when an angel is about
to die, tired of his place in heaven,

the lamps in their ghost-roles lit
of themselves, the essence of all
pretenders, and the unmet lamp-bearing
angels, needy and dark, supposed it day.

The Piano Silker

They have shot an arrow into the sea,
a sea-mark, drawn to a tensile strain,
now visible to sound its thin wooden sound,
its unbraced, silvery treble.

Was the journey endured by the instrument
languid and trifling, half-listening
like the sawed-off half of the moon
to understand past sound?

One piece of lime-tree, doe-skin,
two towers, one inside the other,
steel overspun with copper,
candela flash of candle-power.

The sea sends its tides up
to push the river back against the weir:
a saint-bell in a natural hand position
calls to the sea's first wave.

And immediately her finger leaves a key,
its shallow touch falls back
by its own weight, tide-rips
in the tide-race about gravelly islands.

Roseweather

Where your waters will be
in ocean or cloud
in a little while

it could look lavender-grey,
like the blueing of flowers
as they age, provided for,

loosened in their soil-hold,
their briar-necks leaving
a snag of wood

breaking from a lower eye.
The unbroken green of July
was an actual trail of fire

over rarest sea-shells
and precious stones,
bringing the liveliness

of yellow flowers
to the rent hymen of your soul
outgrowing some form of prayer.

But not a true self-yellow
in its long and open wooing,
guarding your cambrium rings.

Hesterna Rosa

Still has become already,
and yesterday's rose
a red dove, swept away
with a leaf whisk.

The sundial's shadow
falls on nine
with the calmest gesture,
each in its utmost force.

Our city-music
was the singing of a Mass
for the relief of fever,
prefiguring the day

a small landscape
would be fashioned
from your hair's soul-circuit
under glass.

The cool womb
of your body-harp
and the moon as we
begin to see it

in the time-zone of evening;
the moon's voice
meets this moon within you,
brilliant as a forest

around the dusky nightmare
of the house, where the musicians
are being forced to play
death more sweetly.

Telesphorous

The earth complains, her body
stiffens like a lock, some pulled the mountain
so powerfully towards themselves.

In that part of the rainbow
where the most water is attracted,
the water felt its hyacinth colour
as a very dark jewel.

The daughter of the river
adjusted her heart to the season,
a certain darkness existed between
the swan rider and the water hider.

Those deities of moonshine
whose bodies overlap
were separated from each other
by centuries as it were.

Two marsh birds,
when the pouring-places
flooded the daytime world
from the night-world,

asked the god of convalescence,
what kind of rescue this is?
The old thatched cathedral
showed three heavens

through the remains of a bed.
The bee-nymph called iron
or star by the Greeks
made this secular weather-cast —

a year of rest for the earth.

She is in the Past, She has this Grace

My mother looks at her watch,
as if to look back over the curve
of her life, her slackening rhythms:
nobody can know her, how she lost herself
evening after evening in that after,
her hourly feelings, the repetition,
delay and failure of her labour
of mourning. The steps space themselves
out, the steps pass, in the mists
and hesitations of the summer,
and within a space which is doubled
one of us has passed through the other,
though one must count oneself three,
to figure out which of us
has let herself be traversed.

Nothing advances, we don't move,
we don't address one another.
I haven't opened my mouth
except for one remark,
and what remark was that?
A word which appeases the menace
of time in us, reading as if
I were stripping the words
of their ever-mortal high meaning.

She is in dark light, or an openness
that leads to a darkness,
embedded in the wall
her mono-landscape
stays facing the sea
and the harbour activity,
her sea-conscience being ground up
with the smooth time of the deep,
her mourning silhouetted against

the splendour of the sea
which is now to your left,
as violent as it is distant
from all aggressive powers
or any embassies.

And she actively dreams
in the very long ending of this moment,
she is back in her lapping marshes,
still walking with the infinite
step of a prisoner, that former dimension
in which her gaze spreads itself
as a stroke without regarding you,
making you lower your own gaze.

Who will be there,
at that moment, beside her,
when time becomes sacred,
and her voice becomes an opera,
and the solitude is removed
from her body, as if my hand
had been held in some invisible place?